Smiling Through the Pain

Smiling Through the Pain Copyright © July 2021
By Deneen J. Majors

Published in the United States of America by
ChosenButterflyPublishing LLC

www.cb-publishing.com

All rights reserved under International Copyright Law. Contents and/or cover may not be reproduced, distributed, or transmitted in any form or by any means or stored in a database or retrieval system, without the prior written consent of the publisher and/or authors. Brief quotations may be used in literary reviews

Unless otherwise indicated, all Scripture quotations are taken from the King James Scriptures marked KJV are taken from the KING JAMES VERSION (KJV): KING JAMES VERSION, public domain.

or New International Versions of the Bible. NIV®. Copyright © 1973, 1978, 1984, 2011 by Biblica, Inc.™ Used by permission of Zondervan. All rights reserved worldwide. www.zondervan.com The "NIV" and "New International Version" are trademarks registered in the United States Patent and Trademark Office by Biblica, Inc.™

ISBN: 978-1-945377-18-1
Printed in the United States of America
May 2021

Proceed with Caution!

When the Holy Spirit led me to write this book, at first, I just wrote what was on my heart. It was like getting it out of my system was a way for me to express the pain and agony I was going through. It was as if I was being led through my ups and downs as a way to work through it all and visualize where my life had gone off track. It was more painful than I cared to realize. I felt like, *Lord, can you just take it away or take me away? I don't want to love him no more. I don't want to feel this anymore. Why do I have to keep going through this? Why me, Lord? What did I do to deserve this type of hurt? I was good to him and his family. Why?*

And it was at that moment that it all made sense. I had to grieve because of the grief I gave God. I was out of alignment. All the times I allowed that man to manipulate me to get his way, doing things I did not want to do just to keep peace in our home ... well, that grieved God. Even though I felt I was doing what was best for our family, God was not pleased. But because of His grace and His mercy, God still protected me. My saying no was a big deal in our home. Even those times when I did whatever he asked of me it made no difference ... he was still very unfaithful. I blocked it all out.

People would inform me of what he was doing and whom he was seeing, but I refused to be that crazy person checking phones and riding around looking for him. I just wanted my family. So

I just blocked it out. I became very distant and to be honest I was just going through the motions. I had these kids and I just wanted them to have what I didn't and that was a mom and dad together in the home raising them as a team. Little did I know I was creating more damage than good. My kids went through hell. And they have scars to this day. Though I believed I was doing right by them, I caused them pain and it bothered me.

Then, one day, I guess someone new caught his eye AGAIN so he made a big deal about something small and moved out. This time I did not protest. Although he still came around for a while, I later found out that it was all part of a greater plan he had devised. I just went along with it. Again he was stringing me along, but I allowed it.

Proceeding with caution only became a thing while writing this book. Even as the words flowed through my fingers, I was still very cautious about what I would say because I did not want anyone to look at him wrongly or judge him. As if I can control any of that. Even though I was treated unfairly, I was still protecting him because no one knew him the way I knew him. There are secrets we hold for each other that will never be revealed.

I could blast him, but how would that help anyone heal? So to all of you looking for the scoop, it's not here! Here is where I began to heal. The most difficult part of healing is letting go. Once I learned that my love language and his love language are different it all made sense. Understanding each other became easier on my end. Telling him to stop confusing me by saying he loved me and he would always take care of me split me inside. But the Holy Spirit says, "He is telling you the truth. The only problem is he is incapable of loving just you because of the emotions you draw out of him. It is way too much for him to handle. Everyone else is easy but you, Deneen. The power in you is so strong that you make him see himself and his true calling. It makes him uneasy. Glory to God! There is a power and a peace in you ... so the reason you were proceeding with caution was because you are responsible. You know that you have a responsibility to lift up God's people not tear them down. Look how you prayed for those who mocked you, taunted you and called you out of your name. Look how you wished no harm would come to them; how you asked God to bless them and to have mercy on them. That was not by mistake but truly by design."

Proceed with caution. As you read this book, proceed with caution. There is an anointing on these pages ... proceed with caution. Word curses hurled at the author return to the sender immediately in the name of Jesus! Every word meant to be an insult was turned into a steppingstone, which caused her elevation in the name of Jesus!

Thank You God!

Smiling Through The Pain

By Deneen J. Majors

Dedication

To my friend Deetra Chanee Foreman It's hard to imagine you not being here. The problem is I'm still looking for inbox messages, tags and text messages from you because it seems so unreal. One thing that stuck out about you was your smile and how no matter what you were dealing with in your life no matter how much pain it caused you, you continued to smile right through it. Thank you for the long-needed conversations and the laughs. I know you have them cracking up in Heaven. I love and miss you so much, but we will always have Norbit, The Klumps and The Color Purple. Rest easy sis 10/14/1975 to 4/14/2021

To my girl Travonnia "Tinkabell" Stewart-Phelps you left us way too soon. In writing this part your face kept popping up. You endured so much dealing with Sarcoidosis that it's a blessing you kept it together as good as you did. No matter the pain you kept on smiling. I love you lil sis for still working to keep the ladies and family together even when you did not feel your best. You are another great example of smiling through your pain. I love you and if you see Grandma Eva tell her Kelly and I are gonna bake another strawberry cake and share with Uncle Vonnie this time. Rest in power 9/13/1975-3/23/2021

To my children who pushed me through my pain I love you. I don't know what I would have done if it were not for me wanting better for us all.

There are so many who have inspired me over the years so to those who were there, this is for you. I love you.

And last but definitely not least to the only wise God I say thank you. Thank you for placing in me everything I need to succeed. Thank you for protecting me, providing for me, guiding me and propelling to my next. I am so grateful to be called the daughter of a King. I am so thankful that you saved me, snatched from the path of death many, many times. I don't know where I would be If I did not have you Father in the name of Jesus. I pray that you allow this account of a part of my life to help others. You live in me…I am a daughter of the King! King Jesus. Amen

Table of Contents

Dedication 9
Smiling through the Pain 13
Smiling 3 17
Smiling 4 21
Smiling 5 23
Smiling 6 25
Smiling 7 27
Smiling 8 29
Smiling 9 31
Smiling 10 33
Smiling 11 35
Smiling 12 37
Smiling 13 39
Smiling 14 43
Smiling 15 47
Smiling 16 49
Smiling 17 51
Smiling 18 53
Smiling 19 55
Smiling 20 57
Smiling 21 61
Smiling 22 65
About the Author 71

Smiling through the Pain

Have you ever loved someone so much that you could not see they never loved you? There's no way they could have thought that the lies and horrible treatment of you were justified with some money, diamonds and a bunch of cars that always needed some work. But being who I am I never complained and was always grateful for what was given. I appreciate whatever someone does for me. But here's where it gets a little tricky ... painful. Allowing someone's spirit to overpower you can take you out! Yep! I thought I had made it. I actually thought I was done and was moving forward in my life with my businesses. I thought God heard my prayers, removed everything that was not like Him and I was on a roll. Then he started being nice to me again and having meaningful conversations and I allowed him back into my circle only to be fooled again. Over the years he dangled the same carrot over my head about marriage and family and I would fall right back into old habits. What was the pain? Well, we will get to that, but first allow me to tell you a little more about me.

I cannot say that I had a horrible childhood. I can't even say that growing up I was unloved. That is the furthest from the truth. Everyone loved me. So they say. I was a great kid. I did as I was told. My mom may have spanked me once or twice, my Grandma once and no one else except Ma Dozier got me for fighting on her porch, but that was to help one of my cousins. I was never suspended from school or anything like it. Quite the contrary, I was actually the teacher's pet so to speak. I was as tough as a boy but just as cutesy as a girl.

Life didn't get real complicated until I got grown or thought I was grown. Had a couple boyfriends but not one of them can say I cheated on them. All of them, but one, cheated! And at this point, when I look back, the first thought that came to mind was, *What is wrong with me? Why is this happening to me?* I will answer that later. You see, I was at a different place in my life. I just wanted a man to treat me special. Love me, protect me and share his life with me and just me. If you notice I did not say marry me because here's the reason ... I was scared.

Over the years, in every relationship there was something or someone in the way. Drugs, alcohol, and in most cases women and a combination of all the above mentioned. It was always something I did that made them stray. They didn't like the relationship I had with my mother. They said I worked too much. I was told that I thought I knew everything because I went to "Nawfuk" State (translation Norfolk State). It was always something. Nothing I did was ever right. After all these years, it's still the same mess. You see, those who are not right will try everything they can to justify their wrongs.

It does not matter how good, how loyal, how faithful you are, they will find a way to discredit you. You can't allow them to. You cannot sit and wallow in self-pity. Remember earlier I asked what was wrong with me? Well, the answer is simple... There is nothing wrong with me and there is nothing wrong with you either. The only thing wrong is we chose to love the wrong person without checking to see if they were capable of loving us in return. In order for them to love us, they must first love themselves. When you can be a liar, and deceive people who give you loyalty and respect, how can you even say you love yourself?

My first mistake in my last relationship was giving away my power to someone who never deserved my attention. I must admit I did experience some growth with him. He said I had to get my own place to be with him not living at home. So I did. I was comfortable! I did not want to own a salon before meeting him. I was comfortable. Now I have had three. His level of control and manipulation was tested one day though. I was presented with an opportunity to get my second salon and he was against the move. He told me if I moved he was leaving me. I heard God say, "MOVE, DENEEN!" And I did. And guess what … he helped! He did not leave and, to tell the truth, I was glad he didn't leave. I did not want him to go even though I had not been treated normally.

I know how a person is supposed to treat someone they say they love and care for so I waited with hopes of finally getting that love. Even a little love would have been okay. It was like I was under a spell and I finally figured it out. I don't like to lose! For years I heard, "You deserve better. You deserve someone who can love you," and in my mind I thought he loved me because that's what he always told me. It's the showing me part that had me stumped. But God has been working in me. Can't nobody love you like God can.

Smiling 3

Being around positive, uplifting people who don't mind being transparent caused me to look at life differently. I never thought I would ever be able to deal with life the way I can now. I was very afraid to be alone so I allowed some things to go on in my life that truly upset God. My salon business began to slow up, and every business or opportunity I tried never amounted to much and my relationship was almost non-existent. But I kept holding on, holding on to my hopes of it being more.

There is a scripture, Phillippians 4:13, that reads *I can do all things through Christ who gives me strength.* And because I truly believe that, I pulled on God. I knew that to get through this I had to trust Him. I had to pray for strength. I trust the Lord even when I don't understand it ... now. Oh, believe me when I say I have not always been so trusting of God. No, I was never real religious, but I knew in my heart God loved me. I just could not understand how I was supposed to be so loved by God and going through such hard times financially. I gave my tithes, was going to church regularly, but truthfully there was something missing. Have you ever felt that you were doing all things right and nothing went how you felt it should? Like you couldn't catch a break? Did you feel like life had forgotten all about you? If you knew God then, did you feel like God had left you all alone? The truth is God never leaves us. We always leave God.

At times we are so far away that we cannot hear God or see His wonders.

I just could not figure it out. My life was out of alignment and I didn't even know what that meant at that time. *Alignment with what or with whom? What is really going on?* I sank deeper into depression. The smile on my face hid the pain in my heart. There I was, young and what was once full of life was now deflated. I felt as if the world knew my shame. I was just a woman who wanted to give her children a full family unit. We didn't have a dog, but we had plenty of fish until Dad decided to clean the tank, lol. Just wanted to lighten up the mood a little because talking about this always brings up so much pain for me; I did not get it or understand it until my healing began.

What I learned is we were both dealing with some deep-rooted family stuff. I cannot speak about his family stuff because that will be his story to tell. I can only speak on my own personal issues.

Some say that my issues began with my parents' separation, but I can't claim that because I was too young to remember. Some may also say that I have issues because of my dad's inconsistent behavior. But me personally, I can't say that any of that was my issue because I had some awesome father figures that loved me like their own—my grandfather, uncles, my #2 dad Carl and my bonus dad Pop Dozier. I never missed a beat! Every example I saw of a relationship was marriage, but as my cousin Charlene Michelle would say, "Neen, you lived your life looking through rose-colored glasses," and I guess she was right. I always looked for and saw the good in everyone no matter what others would say. I can't even count the number of times people asked me what I was doing with "Mister." I would get upset and defend him. *Why are they asking me that? What's wrong with him?* I could see no wrong. I was completely blind. To me he was everything. And that angered God. *You shall have no other gods before Me* - Exodus 20:3.

I began to truly see my life. I had let my Father down and I am not talking about my biological father either. The once bubbly, vibrant, upbeat woman was now looking for the first exit out of life. I felt as if the world was laughing at me. There I was, one of God's special flowers, and I was being neglected. I wasn't watered, pruned or cared for. That would soon change.

Smiling 4

When my Grandma Eva would say, "A drunk mouth speaks a sober tongue," it would always baffle me. I thought it was some type of riddle. It wasn't until I got older that it made sense. Have you ever been intoxicated or been around someone intoxicated and they say really nice things or really mean things? Well, for me it would be a combination of the two. When they said really nice things it was from the heart, but so were the really mean things. The words spoken are the true feelings they harbor toward themselves and others about themselves or others. Never take those words lightly, or, as my Grandma used to say, don't take those words with a grain of salt. Listen to those words because out of the mouth the heart speaks! Alcohol gives one a false sense of security, boldness and courage. That was truly one of the hardest lessons for me. Hearing the person I loved so much build me up and tear me down in the same conversation. Had it not been for the Lord on my side there is no telling where I would be right now. Facts!

We have got to learn to hear what is said and understand what is not being said. Listen close and listen deep. But don't get too far in. If we listen good enough the voice within picks up and kicks in! That voice can only be saying one of two things: love or hate. If it is a message of love, it comes from God. A message of hate does not come from God. I am not giving anything any credit here, but you must know your source. I know where all my help comes from. Understand this ... there was a time when

I didn't have a clue. I thought it was all about me. I did the work. I grew my businesses. I created this and made that, but one day it all came crashing down. I was then shown that *nothing is impossible without God but with God all things are possible* - Matthew 19:26.

So whether you have been the "drunk mouth" or have been the victim of its spewing, I'm here to tell you that it is okay. Not one of us is perfect. We have all fallen short of God's grace, but He is a forgiving God. He just wants us to acknowledge Him, ask for forgiveness, believe, have faith, love, be kind and trust.

Smiling 5

Who do you feel safe talking to? Why do I ask? Well, I ask because there was a time when I felt talking to those closest to me about what I was dealing with was best for me. Having that human verbal interaction made it seem like I was getting the answers I needed. It was connected to a feeling. The problem is not everyone can keep a secret. When they can't and it burns a hole in their tongue, just know they have to spill the tea. Now, there was this one time I confided in someone I thought was like a sister and she ran that mouth pillow talking to her boyfriend. This joker walks up to me and says, "We were worried about you."

I said, "Excuse me?" My heart sank. I thought, *Wow, I wonder what else he knows.* I felt a little embarrassed. I have never told anyone her secrets. I felt like I had been hit in the face with a kickball. All I could do to keep from crying was to just smile and try to play it off like I had no idea what he was talking about. It sort of made me wonder how much of my business has been discussed while they were pillow talking.

We really should not do that. I mean seriously. First of all, your mate will look at your friends differently and may say something, especially once they get liquored up. It's embarrassing. If you are called to be a good friend then be that. Right now I have one person outside of my sister that I can share with and she is the best! Human contact is good, but I also learned that anything I don't want repeated I take straight to God! God is the best confidant! I call on Him in the name of Jesus and allow the Holy Spirit to speak and pour into me.

I pull out my journal and I write. I write everything that pops up in my head, everything I hear, and it's in my own voice. I used to think the voice would be a loud, deep, audible sound, kind of animated, but it wasn't. I was shocked. A friend said, "When you pray and ask God for answers, you have to be ready to record what you hear." That's so true. When I pray and I'm having quiet moments alone, I hear the voice and it is so clear. I have my journal ready also.

I never knew how important a journal would become to my life. A friend suggested I start one. Over the years I have received many instructions from God, but because I was not ready to hear I missed a lot. How many times have you heard the answers to your questions clear as if the person was sitting across from you but you did not write down what you heard? Well, I can say this has happened to me many times. After hearing a friend mention it on a prayer call I started to become more serious about my journaling. I talk to God and I write.

God keeps the best secrets.

Smiling 6

Loving yourself is so important. At times we tend to forget about ourselves because we are so wrapped up in our families, jobs, businesses, churches, etc. Until you love yourself it is impossible to love others. I see it many times when we are going through and we don't take care of ourselves. We don't care how we look on the outside because the inside is so messed up. My Uncle Clarence used to say, "Just 'cause you doing bad doesn't mean you gotta look bad. Fix yourself up!" And he meant it too. I always felt better once I got it together. Again, that was a way I was able to camouflage my hurt. I covered it up in labels!

I was raised in a very loving environment. My family was close. All my aunts, uncles, and cousins always came over to our house. So we always had a house full. My entire street growing up had twelve of the most amazing families I had ever had the pleasure of meeting. Two houses had two different families, but I count them all. I learned something from many of them. And to this day we are still a close-knit unit. We may have all gone on to different places but we will always have Virginia Avenue. Most of us who are living are still quite close. And we still love one another.

We knew exactly what the old African proverb "It takes a village to raise a child" meant. My block in my neighborhood was our village. Everyone took care of everyone. The neighbors, teachers, bus drivers, everyone had the authority to correct you.

We respected the elders of the neighborhood. So many discount and disregard our elders now forgetting that many of them paved the way for us. *You shall stand before the gray head and honor the face of an old man and you shall fear your God. I am Lord!* - Leviticus 19:32KJV

I was talking about love and loving others for a reason. Some people don't have positive examples of love from family, friends, neighbors ... anybody. But we expect them to be able to be these great examples of love when many of them are hurting and have no clue what real love is and couldn't recognize it if it sat in their lap.

What I'm now learning to do is to pay close attention to what is NOT being said. The truth is in what is not spoken. Use your head and not your heart yet. You don't have to be cold or insecure. Nor must you be messy and disrespectful. Just cultivate your relationship with God. Get to know Him and watch how it all will work out for your good. Love is a beautiful thing. I know because I feel it every day I wake up.

Smiling 7

One morning, while on The Lifeline Prayer Call, which is a call founded by my mentor, I heard one of the women say, "Your breakthrough is on the other side of your pain." I was like, *Okay...* Then she said, "You have to go through some stuff in order to find your purpose." Now, I know I had heard this before, but for some reason this time it felt different. I'm sitting and listening and all that comes to mind is, *I don't like pain. The feelings of rejection, not being good enough, unloved in a relationship and just a lot of horrible stuff running all through me and you're telling me that this is part of my process! Really!*

I could not stop crying. *In my mind all I could think was, What did I do to deserve this? I'm a good person. I go to church. I treat people with kindness.* And the Holy Spirit said, "Yes you do, daughter, but all those things are just a small part of your greater purpose."

I was an absolute mess. I did not want to feel any more hurt. I wanted to just hide myself from the world so that I would never feel hurt again. But through scripture reading and fellowshipping with others, I found comfort in my times of need. I know that God is faithful. I know that trouble don't last always. I know that the pain I felt will help make me stronger. I also know the pain was not for me. I had to go through to be able to help someone else.

Smiling 8

Who am I to judge? That is a question I often ask myself, now but there was a time that question never crossed my mind. I was someone, many years ago, who thought I could look at a person or be around them and know all I needed to know. And that was oh, so wrong.

I judged everything. I was a know-it-all spoiled brat, but I didn't look for any handouts. I got it all on my own ... so I thought. If a person wasn't "grinding" (hustling/working hard) like me, I could not understand why not. I never factored in that we are all at different levels, we have our own set of obstacles/distractions and not to mention our goals, dreams, visions and expectations are not the same. I was called arrogant, mean, and snotty with no regard for other people's feelings. I knew better. I was young and my head had gotten too big!

Being an only child growing up, I always had to be the best at everything so that I wouldn't get lost in the crowd at the bottom. I had the best handwriting. I could spell better than most of my class. I was also great in math. Great dancer and singer. Captain of my cheerleading squad for every team I cheered for. Wow! I just went for it! And yes, I was judged. All my life I heard what was said even by those who claimed to love me so much. But it made me stronger. Folks would be surprised at the things I know I have been judged on even as a young girl, but I never allowed it to change who I was or who I would become as I got older. I received a lot of snide remarks because so many women were envious of my mother. And to be honest my mom says she doesn't know why she always had so many problems with women.

My mom gave birth to me two days after her 18th birthday. And yes, she married my father. Some thought she would end up on welfare with a house full of babies, but her goal was to prove them wrong. My mom was on welfare for six months and she said that $201 wasn't enough to take care of me so she got a job. My father was a musician. Yes! A local celebrity, lol. The folks in Oceanview loved The Blockbusters of Roanoke Rapids! It didn't pay enough and they couldn't get it together. My parents separated because they were on different wavelengths. I love them both and they love me.

My mom is an amazing woman. She didn't want to hurt my grandfather by making me move with her because she saw how bad he cried when my cousin moved away to New York. So, she allowed me to stay. My mom was and still is a very active part of my life and my kids' lives. We are thankful for her and my POP ... she remarried. There is joy after the pain! After all the nasty things people would say about my mom I had to learn that it don't matter how others see you. It only matters how God sees us. Our ultimate goal in life is to please God.

Smiling 9

Words are so powerful. There was a time when I did not understand how much power lies within our words. As children many of us have more than likely chanted this phrase more than we care to remember: sticks and stones may break my bones but words will never hurt me—lies! I have said some mean things and been told some pretty mean things that tore me apart and did the same for many others. Words can be soothing, calming, loving, caring and all that good gushy stuff. But they can also be rude, sharp, cutting, mean, angry, hateful, malicious and downright nasty. In one breath I have been told I'm loved, I'm beautiful, I'm a good mother with a good heart then comes the but ... but you ain't no type of woman. I'm like, *What the heck does that even mean?* I was so confused. I did everything a "wife/mother" did except one thing ... give up that money! I have a strong support system. My family is always very supportive of me, but just because I have backup it does not make me less of a woman. It just means I am blessed. Instead of being happy that I had some people to call on who were willing to help me, they tore me down with their words.

Not everyone is blessed to have that type of support. So they don't know how to receive it. Their pride gets in the way. Many people are too prideful to ask for help from family. My family was not raised like that. I remember seeing my grandparents paying rent, mortgages, utilities, feeding folks and heard countless stories of their good deeds to their neighbors. They moved whole families into their already crowded home with no second thought. Pride comes before the fall. Insecurity will make people do some crazy stuff.

Some people you hook up with want to be your only lifeline. I have seen them cut their mate off from family and friends. That is how they are able to control you emotionally. Thankfully that did not happen to me.

I began to really pray and ask God why and what I needed to do because I felt like I was sinking. Nothing I did was right. Arguing and fussing all the time and it was literally for no reason at all. I heard some say, "You have to get your heart right." I was like, *Lord, what is wrong with my heart?* I had given my all to my family, our home and salon. I didn't know what to do or where to begin.

A friend said, "Go look up Psalm 51:10." It said *Create in me a clean heart, Oh God, and renew a right spirit within me daily.* I was like, *Oh, okay.* So I did it. Every day.

Asking God to clean our heart is a great way to start recovering. When your heart is pure, you see things clearer. We are not perfect, remember. We all have some things that could use work. We have to use our words to uplift, encourage and inspire others, not tear them down.

Smiling 10

Even though I knew in my heart what he was doing when he was out in the streets, I blocked it out. I ain't checking no boyfriend's phone or riding around looking for him. That's just crazy to me. If I have to do all that then it's way too much. Truth be told, I could feel through the lies and the deceit that he was only honest when he was angry or around his friends. It was like a yo-yo. You do know what a yo-yo is, right? It's like a ball with a string attached that you kind of throw out and retrieve with a flick of your wrist. One minute I'm loved then the next minute I'm no earthly good. If the kids didn't love me so much he would've gotten rid of me. That hurt me. But I loved my babies ... all of them. And my goal was to pour as much love into each of them as I possibly could.

He would apologize with something material or money and we move on like it never happened. It was more about the kids for me, but I couldn't understand any of this. I had never been this way in any relationship before. I had no problem cutting ties. This time was different. Something had us tied together. Then, after many years had passed, one day it just hit me... This was never about him or me. This was about our children. You see we all have these generational curses passed down. Once I began to tap in, things began to become clearer. God used me! It took me years to grasp this. My children are all extremely blessed. All the times I felt he had used me God stepped in and took over! What man tried to do for bad God used for His Glory! God kept me even in my darkest hour. Even when I felt used, abused and unappreciated God kept me. It may seem like all hope is gone, but I promise you this, you are not alone. God's promises have kept me sane through all of this. I am eternally grateful.

Smiling 11

Hurt people hurt people. Ain't that what they say? Angry people, at some point in their lives, have gone through something very painful. Many don't know how to deal with it so they mask the pain. Not just angry people. I meant to say many people. There are some walking around carrying hurt from over 20, 30, 40, 50+ years ago. It's true. Some still carry the hurt, the pain and the shame of their past. Many don't know where to begin to heal. And there are those who feel unworthy of a healing.

There I was with my old bubbly self just floating through life on a cloud. But all around me was discourse and discouragement. I could see it and feel it at times but fought hard not to fall prey to it. I lost that battle in many years to come because it became too much to deal with. I shut myself off from the world. I went to work and I took care of my family. I cared way too much about what others had to say. Not only that, I also wanted to prove that I was the best woman, lover, mom, cook ... just the best choice all around. And I'm sure I was but to the wrong person.

Now that was a real gut punch! And listen, some of you may get the same or a similar revelation. And there is nothing wrong with that. Who we are designed to attract we attract. It's not about how much money you make or how much you spend on the person—true love conquers all. If they belong with you, you will have them even if you have nothing.

At times, a person is dealing with so much that they cannot receive the goodness of those who truly care about them. Again, it's okay. That is not your problem. You tried, now let go. I know it seems easier said than done and, trust me, I know firsthand about this. But God! Lord knows I can tell you all about this kind of hurt. The kind of hurt when they play with your heart. Stand your ground. It's not them; it is a trick of the enemy. Press on. You will have to do a complete detox—mind, body and spirit. Fruits, vegetables, herbs, water and a lot of soul-searching. I made it through simply trusting God. My children, my sisters, family and friends have all stood with me throughout my tests and my trials and I am grateful. I just have to remember that I am royalty, a child of the most high God, and never deserve to be treated any less than that. No one should be called a bitch by their man ever, especially when you are not exhibiting that type of behavior. No woman or man should have to deal with anything like that. You are special, especially to God. When you feel you are not appreciated, it's time to address it. Don't just wait for it to change. It may never. If there is no change, then move on. What God has for you is for you.

Smiling 12

Forgiveness is for you not them. When I first heard this, I was like, *I don't want to forgive him! He put me through too much! I wasted so many years for nothing!* I was so angry! I didn't want to forgive him; I wanted him punished for wasting my time. Then this dropped on me... "Don't you want me to forgive you, daughter?" I cried like a baby. We want God to forgive us for all our wrongs, but we want to hold people to account for what they do to us. I did not see it like that. I was truly thinking it ain't the same thing because God has so much more power than us. But forgiveness is the same for all. In order to move forward we have to drop some stuff. This was huge for me. Over the years, I had held on to a lot of painful memories. My mentor told us to jot down the names of those we felt had wronged us. Go back as far as you can because you may need to unlock some things. She was like, "There may even be some things you need to forgive yourself for, so write your name too." I was like *Man, this could take all night.* But when she said, "What about God? Are you upset with God about anything?" I was like, *I gotta go deeper!* I got so into it I had a lot of names. Some say write out what you forgive them for being specific. Then burn it. Burn it up!

Now, some of you are looking at this like, *Forgive them? Huh! Yeah right. Next you are going to say, "Pray for them."* And guess what? You are correct! Ding! Ding! Ding! You win! Pray for them. When I found out I had to pray for those who had wronged me and pray for my enemies, it was extremely hard. It was harder than giving birth. I had to pray for people who obviously hated me... That was if I wanted to be healed. I had to make it my personal business to ask God to bless my enemies and my haters and to have mercy on them. I know that elevation and promotion comes from God so I have to stay in my lane. I can feel the power of God over my life and I also know that my reaction to situations matters.

So when you hear people say forgiveness is for you, it means in order to get what God has in store for your life you must be able to forgive those who have wronged you. That does not mean you have to forget. No, you have to remember so you can recognize it if you see it again. But don't remember in order to keep throwing it up in their faces every time you have a disagreement. Forgive, pray and move on.

Smiling 13

Do you know what it's like to become invisible? I have to ask because right now that is how someone is feeling. I felt somewhat ashamed after I had an unnecessary falling out with a sometime client. She was one who was very demanding and even after I'd given her more attention than deserved she flipped out on me.

One day, she came in to be serviced. No, she did not have a formal appointment. She was a "can I come in today" client and of course I always said, "Yes!" I always gave it my best shot to get everyone in when they needed to see me. This particular day, she was already agitated when she came in ... late. I ran out of something I needed and when my sis Diane was on her way to me, ahead of her time, she asked if I needed anything and I did. I paid over the phone and Diane made the stop to get my products. When Diane arrived, I instructed her to go straight to the shampoo bowl. Oh now, Lord, why did I do that? Even though I am the one aware of all the scheduling, doing all the work, and aware of everyone's time, that lady got angry, but she did not show it. She sat for a few moments then told me she would reschedule. We exchanged heartfelt pleasantries because again I love all my clients and go above and beyond for each of them. I am very appreciative and thankful. I am grateful that they each have chosen me.

This one here was a firecracker ready to pop and I was unaware. She called my phone but it had to be the Holy Spirit that allowed that call to go straight to voicemail. This lady left the nastiest messages I have ever received. And I bet you can guess what happened next. Yes, I called her, so if that's what you were thinking then you are on the right page! And it was not good. This lady called me all kinds of names. Started calling me stupid because she knew a lot of my personal business. Some folks close to me were talking. She was saying some really hurtful things that went far beyond her feeling I had taken Diane in front of her. The conversation was downright disgusting. She talked about my ex, my kids, my everything. But what got me was this... She said, "All your friends who you think are your friends are all sitting around talking about you, laughing at you and calling you stupid because that's what you are. You are a stupid bitch!" She said it with such venom that it bit me and it stung! She cursed me and me being who I once was I cursed her back! I cursed her out something terrible. That's when it really went wrong because she didn't tell her child the truth. She played the innocent role and I was ready to go to jail. It was bad.

Now, you may ask why I shared that incident; well, it was a part of my life and it was what caused me to disappear. Remember me saying I just didn't know who to talk to? Well, this is also why. I was dying inside. I was fighting a losing battle because I did not want anyone to know how things were in my "relationship." I smiled even though the pain was so severe. I felt invisible at home and tried to stay invisible in the streets.

I stopped going out and hanging with my "friends" and started to spend even more time with the children. We were already inseparable, but now I relied on them as my shopping partners, my eating buddies, my dates, my hang out partners ... my everything. It was crazy that I left a girlfriend's birthday celebration cookout because her mom said no kids were allowed at the cookout. So I took them shopping and to dinner and that was that. I was used to it. He always sent me out with the kids while he "worked" or "took care of something." No complaints because we used his money well.

What I learned later was I had to have some hangout folks because when your children grow up they don't want to hang with you anymore. They have their own lives and friends. That's when I really found a friend in Jesus. My friend Jesus led me to an awesome bunch of friends/business partners and that's when life was fun again.

Being or simply feeling invisible has so many different levels of definitions. One of my clients told me once that her husband didn't notice her new haircut or new dress until her grandbaby said something. I guess he was so accustomed to her look that anything new he could not see. She was invisible to him. I did not have that problem. He notices everything about me even to this day. Always has something to say good or not so good with his opinionated self, lol. But I have grown so unbothered. It was the grace of God that pulled me out of this. Just trust Him.

Smiling 14

I remember growing up and hearing the grown-ups talking about different things and honestly not giving a real thought to any of their conversations. When you paid too much attention or were caught repeating what you heard, you were called "too grown." I didn't want to be called too grown because no one wanted to be around the child that was too grown. Boy my family would talk about you terribly, lol... I love them. But there was one phrase my uncle Ronald would say and they would all just crack up laughing. "Ain't no fun when the rabbit got the gun." I thought it was because he and I watched a lot of Bugs Bunny and Elmer Fudd! And I would look at them laughing and think to myself, *My uncle is so funny.* I thought he was a comedian making up jokes like Richard Pryor and Redd Foxx who I ain't have no business watching back then with them, but I could keep a secret. I did not understand that there was a message in what he was saying. Time would tell and life would eventually show me just what he meant.

You see, as long as folks are having fun doing others just how they want to do them, being selfish and mistreating them, really not valuing the relationship they have with them, they are good. But the moment the tables turn and the mistreated, disrespected person decides they have had enough and moves on here comes that old thing again. They don't want you but don't want anyone else to have you. Some will say, "Go get you a friend because I moved on," only to slip and call you in the wee hours of the morning or when they are intoxicated spilling their guts. Now that you have found a piece of happiness, here they come. They still play games, though, so don't fall for the banana in the tailpipe. Your season has passed. Keep it moving! Love yourself. Live for yourself. It's time to take back your power. Get back all that was stolen from you ... our hopes, our dreams, our livelihood, our ability to love ourselves and others. Take it all back and press towards the mark! It's time to stop worrying about all that could've, should've or would've been and see life for what it truly is.

We are all gifts from God. We all just use our gifts differently. Some for good and some for evil. We are all created equal. We all have an amazing purpose. It's okay that we get stuck ... we just cannot stay stuck. Do you know what stuck means? I know what it means to me. It's what I was when I started writing this book, stuck in a relationship that could not move forward because of all the weights. The weights were lifted once I surrendered to God. The enemy tricked my mind. Had me believing that I had to have him and I was losing everything. I thought I would fade away and disappear to the world. Jesus! Oh, but once I surrendered to the will of God my elevation began. It was something I had never felt. I had sunk to my lowest point. Almost begging him to tell me why not me. And IT HAD NOTHING TO DO WITH HIM! GOD SAVED ME! GOD RESCUED ME! God plucked me out of an uncomfortable situation and I am eternally grateful.

You may or may not be stuck or have never been in a stuck like state. Your stuck may not be my stuck. It could be relationship related, an addiction, substance abuse, gambling, overeating, or a million other things. Take a moment and define your "quicksand." What has you stuck, if anything, right now?

Smiling 15

"He comforts us so that we may comfort others." That's 2 Corinthians 1:4 KJV. Does that not sound like a real parent, one who takes the time to make you feel better no matter what they may be dealing with? Our comforter is very busy but never too busy to tend to us. How many times have we as parents, as children, as friends, as a family member been too busy to support someone else? It is possible that the storm you have brewing in your life, which God is helping you through, is no match for the storm your sister or brother may be going through? It may be no match for the issues your cousin is facing. It may pale in comparison to the stuff your best friend may have going on in their lives and in all honesty your storm could be greater. But here's where it gets tricky… God is trusting YOU to comfort THEM, not them to comfort you this time. It's your turn to help someone else. Though you may be saying, "I'm always helping others," and that may be true, that's because God trusts you. He knows just who you are in Him and He knows the outcome. No, we don't get it right all the time because we are imperfectly human. But it's in our efforts to do His work that God finds pleasure. Not everyone is receptive. But your obedience is what pleases God most.

Even in your brokenness you can help comfort someone else. This is so true and so real to me. I have been here in this place and it was in my sharing a comforting word with a friend that I found my peace. We all go through, but the difference is many of us go through alone. We cry many nights shedding rivers of tears. But trust me; there is no relief like a release in HIM! We have got to learn to let go and let God be God! So many times I have tried to control the outcome of things and always messed something up. It happens when you don't surrender and fully trust the process to God. It's like you want what you want without understanding that may not be what God has for you. Remember this saying, "If it don't fit, don't force it. Just relax and let it go?" How many of us really live by it? How often do we try to force the outcome? This is where you come in. When you have been here and God helped you through, it is now your turn to give back. It's your time to be a comforter.

Smiling 16

Have you ever been in a relationship and all you wanted was to be with that person together forever? You know, get married, have kids or not, the house, the dog, the cat, goldfish and turtle? While you are being faithful to this person and planning your future in your mind and expressing yourself verbally, they slippin' and slidin' around town doing any and everything but accusing you of being the cheater. They constantly question your loyalty.

Let me paint this picture for you. All you do is think about them. You are in love. Before I had children, I had my heart broken many times. After the children, I had my heart broken many times. And what played a part in my heartbreak was me. While I was planning our future, they were planning their right now. Some people just live in the moment and that's okay for them. It's when others are being hurt, abused, disrespected and used that it becomes not okay. We have to make sure we take care of the hearts around us. Yes, you are responsible for the pain you cause. You are born to care but taught to disregard. It is all in the lessons we adapt to our lives. A child with an unloving parent has two choices: 1. To be like their parents or 2. To not be like their parents. That's it. Bottom line. So you are either going to do right by people or not. No one deserves to be mistreated. No one should ever feel unwanted in a relationship. No one should have to question if the person they love actually loves them back.

News flash people: Sex and abuse DOES NOT EQUAL LOVE! Let me break it down a little more. Just because a person gives you their body it does not mean they love you. And sex does not fix anything. It just heightens the hurt. Some cannot perform or get aroused when they are emotionally broken. Your state of mind matters to your overall health. And just because you give them gifts and money it still does not mean you love them. "A monkey will take money even if he has no pockets to put it in." Nathan Majors said it best.

At the end of the day all I'm sharing with you is it is important to treat people accordingly. If you have no desire to love someone as they should be loved, then be kind enough to walk away. We should strive to love as God loves us. We all have our crosses to bear. Yes we all go through, but don't take your frustrations out on innocent people. I'm speaking from a place of love. I have been loved. I have loved. I have lost and I will love again. And it's okay. This is all a part of my process. I truly believe that God is working all around each of us and the love we desire will be right where it's supposed to be. Just keep doing your part. God got the rest.

Smiling 17

We all have heard about the "why" factor and most of the time when we hear "why" we associate it with what drives us daily. For instance, I can say that my why concerns my family. I do what I do so that I can make my own schedule and determine my income. That is one kind of why but not necessarily the why I'm working on getting us through. This why, although they both carry a certain amount of pain, this why is hurtful! I want to know why! This why occurs when things don't go as planned and it seems that we can't get past the hurt until we know why. We ask questions like, "Why would you cheat on me?" "Why would you lie to me?" "Why this?" "Why that?" "Why, why, why?" We have a million questions and no matter what answers we are given, the answer won't help! The pain will just start over. Rejection is hard. Although it is part of our process, rejection can be brutal. But that's how I used to think. And trust me; I have not always looked at rejection the way I do now. No ma'am, this has definitely been a challenge for me. And there are days when I'm still calling on God to pull me through. And I get it that sometimes we are not ready to release it. We are not ready to see the brighter side of things. We want to be mad, sad, hurt, and get sympathy from those we love. I'm just the messenger... That is not who God called us to be.

We were not created to be fearful or to worry. When we worry, nothing changes. When we trust God, there is a chance. Fear is, as they say, false evidence appearing real. So worry and fear are just two roadblocks thrown in our paths to get us off course. Asking why to a question we really don't want the answer to makes the pain more severe. Though you may not want to believe it, it is possible that the person you are in love with may not be who God intended for you. That opportunity that you worked hard for was not meant for you. And so many other things ... not for you. It's okay! Yes! It's okay! We have more chances, more opportunities as long as we live, love, laugh and treat people with kindness. Our reactions to situations and to those around us matter. So let's not focus on the why did it happen; let's focus on how we can turn it around and use it as fuel for our next level.

Smiling 18

We can only receive from where we are. If I'm a positive person, I see mostly from a more positive standpoint; negative people have a very different outlook. It's mainly because of the different experiences in life. I can say that for the most part I have been quite positive but mainly when it seems life is going my way. Ain't that how it always is? We are good as long as we are happy. But the minute something goes wrong we find someone or something to blame.

God gets blamed for a lot of our mess. I'm just telling it like I see it. I am guilty of this just like many of you. Here I am just pressing through this up and down relationship, heartbroken and feeling like it was about to fall out of my chest because it hurt so badly. I knew I was an awesome mate and did not understand why God had allowed it to happen. I blamed God, even though He had nothing to do with it because I had not really let Him in at this point. And by the time I did, it was too late for us but right on time for me. That's when it all clicked. It was not God's fault that I allowed the standards of the world to dictate how my life should be. I had strayed away from the blueprint.

I've often heard that when a man finds a wife he finds a good thing. He kept saying I was his wife, buying me so many rings and having me think he was going to marry me. Then he started saying he was not gonna marry me because of my mom. I'm like, "What?" He kept up with the same lie that I told him my mom said not to marry him. The truth was she said, "Don't get married unless you are truly ready. Marriage is harder to get out than to get into." But conveniently he never remembered that part. I'm not mad though. God knew better than I did and continued to cover me even when I was unaware.

Pay attention to the world but you do not have to conform to its ways. Peter 2:9 says we are chosen! We are royalty! All of us! And I believe it! Many of us haven't been taught how to be royal, chosen, loved, lovable, loyal or kind-hearted. Being kind doesn't make you soft. It makes you human.

Smiling 19

Just when you thought you lost, God does something amazing to show you that you were actually the winner.

Have you ever been in a situation that even when you had given your all it still wasn't good enough? You gave it all you had and it still wasn't enough. That person still wasn't satisfied. I learned the hard way that it is impossible to please someone who cannot tell you what they want. All they can gripe about is what you are not doing or have yet to do. They have no plan written down ... it is mainly in their head. Now you are a mind reader. You spend most of the time confused because just when you think you have it all figured out, they switch up on you again. It is exhausting. It would be so much easier if you had a plan. Habakkuk 2:2 says to write the vision and make it plain. That means create a blueprint that's easy for all to follow. That's how you move ahead. Relationships are partnerships where we learn what we each of us like and don't like. We should be able to ask and answer questions.

Let's get back to the part of feeling like you lost something or someone because they moved on. You didn't lose ... they did you a favor. If you know that you gave your all then you should not feel bad. You did everything a mate was supposed to do. You were faithful, loyal, respectful, loving, caring, giving, etc. and still unappreciated. Then allow me to be the first to say, "Congratulations! You are the winner!" Many times our Heavenly

Father sees our struggles and our pain so when you ask Him to help you, just know, He is on the job. He will help in the way He sees fit. He answers prayers but in His will and in love. Oftentimes we want God to do things our way, but for Him that is not how He operates. Our way may not be what's best for us.

But wait! Here is another lesson: be careful what you pray for because you just might get it. Have you ever heard that? It's true. You prayed for that man or that woman and they turned into a nightmare! You just had to have them. You had to prove to everyone that you were better than the last person they were with, which sounds crazy to me. Who in the world has this kind of time? But anyway, not judging. You do all this crazy, off-the-wall mess and when you get that Tasmanian devil you wish you could put that thing in an ACME can and ship it off to a desert somewhere. They were not designed for you. Now you are miserable and that spirit is all up in you. God is still there awaiting your surrender. You may not have felt His presence because of all the pain; the fighting and the bruising and the apologies. For me, I shiver when I think of how much more pain I would have endured if the Lord had not shown up for me. All the tears I've cried, sleepless nights, headaches, tummy aches, bowel breakdowns and anxiety attacks were all a part of that spirit! That thing will trick you into believing you want to die; that you can't make it! LIES! Lord, I thank You for keeping me. I'm thankful for Your strength. I'm grateful for Your love, God. I'm blessed because of Your grace and Your mercy. So the next time you have an experience where you think you have lost, just thank God for helping you dodge that bullet.

Smiling 20

Some people in this world have things so mixed up that they mixing up others. I see people with religious words and sayings painted on car windows and doors, billboards and buildings, T-shirts, sweatshirts, notebooks, anywhere they can put it to show how holy they are. Don't get me wrong; with any of those we display our affection for God. I wear my holy gear too. But what God wants is not just a material display. He desires an outpouring of our heart. Can we be loving, kind-hearted and respectful towards others? Can you put the needs of others above your own? He desires those who have fallen and are struggling to allow Him to lead them and to lift them up to become non-judgemental, caring and sensitive to the needs of others. Notice I did not say pushovers. You must have a backbone. Being bold is a must. And if you are a pushover, don't worry ... take it one day at a time. Change doesn't happen overnight. We have to be willing to simply trust God. There is a blueprint designed just for you.

I have listened to others preach, teach and speak God's Word for years and that was fine. I learned a lot. It wasn't until I began to read the Bible for myself that I really began to truly get it. I used to think that once you are done living your life the way you want, then you go to church and serve God. That was all I can remember seeing growing up. Parents who have been in the world then decide to return to the church and drag the kids along. They spend morning, noon and night in church worshipping, praying and serving God to the point that the kids run from church when they are old enough. This is the same cycle that continues through generations. I wish I knew then some of what I know now and a life without God ain't worth living!

I read more. I study more. I definitely talk to God way more now than I have ever in all my life. Once I learned that it's not about the church you frequent or the pastor or bishop presiding, a whole new world opened up for me. I don't know every word in the Bible but I am more familiar with it. I miss days of reading it, but I can say that I have gotten better. My life has gotten better. I still go through some things but now that I have a better understanding I can make better choices.

I KNOW MY SOURCE!

I know my source! I know we all have had doubts in our lives about situations, people, places and things. But one day, while I was going through, a friend asked me if I knew my source. I had to think for a minute because truthfully it had not dawned on me at that time. GOD IS MY SOURCE! So I must trust in the Lord with all my heart and not yield to my own understanding. I know whose voice to listen for. I know my God will never leave me; nor will He forsake me. I know that every delay works in my favor. I also know that delayed does not mean denied ... be patient. I know that I am protected daily and I am covered by the blood that Jesus shed for me when He was persecuted to save the world. And I know that I am redeemed!

We must be willing to ask God for the help we need in all aspects of our lives. To be restored daily and forgiven daily is important because we are all imperfect people living in an imperfect world. So what I am saying to you is this. We all fall short. Staying in church all day for 14+ hours won't make me any holier or better than someone in church for an hour or home enjoying Bedside Baptist! A person can live in church and still be as mean and hateful as a rattlesnake! It's about the heart of the person. Going to church does not mean we have a personal relationship with God. I mean, to tell the truth, that was who I used to be. I gave my tithes faithfully but I had no real knowledge of what being a true believer was about. It was all religious rituals with me, doing what I had been taught. But about six years ago, things changed for me. I learned the importance of a clean heart. A clean heart... Let that sink in. Everything starts with a clean heart. Everything.

Smiling 21

This part I'm about to share is a little difficult because it causes me to be a bit more transparent. And we all know that allowing others to know some very intimate details about you can make you a target, but still, I am being led by the Holy Spirit to share.

As a hairstylist in business for 20+ years, I have experienced some of life's greatest and harshest moments. I have had some amazing weeks and then there were those weeks where I felt not only did the clients leave me but Jesus Himself had taken some time off as well. I felt so alone. My home life was a mess and stressful and I could feel the weight of the world on my shoulders. What's crazy is I blamed everyone and everything, not ever seeing the part I played in this entire mess. I was not humble at all. I knew of God and was familiar with Jesus. Had not heard much about the power of the Holy Spirit and I thought the people shouting were hilarious. Speaking in tongues sounded made up and I was one to say, "It does not take all of that." I quickly learned that it takes all that and more…

My second salon business was failing tremendously and to be honest I was sinking deep into debt and depression. A restaurant purchased my building and I had the nerve to be upset because I had to move out. There was a young lady who had a salon across the street and she invited me to come and be a part of her salon family. I'm not gonna lie, this lady had so much God in her that she gave pieces of Him to all who came in contact with her. Her name was Carla G and though the G stands for Graham, in my eyes it means Great Woman of God! She was a gift to all of us. I can promise you that it was not an accident that I ended up at her salon. That was truly by design. God had to allow me to see some things about myself and about Him. I am so grateful to Carla G for allowing the Lord to use her in so many ways. Back then I never gave God the glory for my creative ability and talents in my career. I got big-headed! But once I got knocked off my high horse and dragged through the mud by my toenails I realized that God is the beginner and the finisher of it all. Everything that I have, that I am, and what's to become comes from GOD!

I lost so many clients that I was contemplating getting a nine-to-five job! I know what you're thinking ... now why would I just be so willing to give up on my career? Well, I was so far behind in my bills at home trying to keep the salon open that I nearly lost my house several times. I had to rely on the kids' dad to pull me out of that jam. I tried many different things to keep the money coming, but nothing was really working like I felt it should have. I was doing okay; then I got sick. Sick, losing clients and feeling sorry for myself. I was so scared. I had to find a job.

There I was in my early 40s without a resume and no clue where to begin to start one, feeling broke, busted and disgusted. Who would've thought that at this age this was my reality? In the hair industry, the slow months last way too long and have killed businesses for decades. I truly believe that even through all of this, I have been blessed. Blessed with a lot of help from God and His Angels. In 15 years, I survived three foreclosures, sleeping in the dark with my children and being without running water because of my pride. I did not want to ask for help unless it was truly a life-or-death situation, never wanted to be looked at as helpless. I knew that if I could do a lot of hair, we would be fine. That worked only some of the time.

I read somewhere a quote that said, "Find something and sell it." I don't remember who said it, but it stuck with me. One day, I received a message from a friend about a product and I did not look at it for six months. After my life-saving operation I had issues going to the bathroom and it came to me that the product she shared with me could possibly help me. I reached out and yep! It did! Not only did it free my bowels, it also freed up some debt! I joined that company and never looked back! Joining Total Life Changes has turned out to be more than just me being a part of a product company. I have this great big family of brothers and sisters and a bunch of mommas and daddies telling us how to get to work in the business and grow. I have grown in faith due to my partnership with The Lifeline Prayer Call that was founded by my mentor Lenika Scott and I am grateful for her constantly pushing me and challenging me to grow ... to get outside of myself and get out of my own way. We all need someone like that. And I am thankful that I have some sisters by blood and love that have pushed and pulled me out of my dead place.

I was given a new life and a new chance to live that was designed just for me. No more living my life trying to satisfy others. All my life that's exactly how I lived. I just wanted to do what was right and do as I was told. That attitude nearly destroyed me because I had someone who did not value my sacrifice. And once I got my life back I could actually see where I had gone off track. You may have felt that way before and I'm here to tell you it's not the end of the world. You're life's not over ... your life is just beginning, AGAIN! FRESH START!

Smiling 22

Your Demons Have a Name Too!

So often we judge the lives and actions of others forgetting that not one of us is perfect. You may notice that I write a lot about being judged. I know what it's like to always have my name coming out of someone's mouth and not always in a good way. As a young girl, I was judged. I have heard people say really horrible things about me, my mom and my grandma but I won't name them because that is not the focus of this book. They said that my grandma thought I was better than the other children. They said I wouldn't amount to anything and I was a spoiled brat. I would end up on welfare with a bunch of "damn churn" is what they said…

I was teased because I was raised by "old people". One person even said I smelled like mothballs because of my grandparents. It hurt at the time but I had tough skin. We were just kids and I know that I didn't smell funny because my mommy purchased every fragrance Avon had—lol—just to make sure of it. Mothballs my dear aunt fanny, lol! I never forgot that. I stored it and that's probably why I'm obsessed with expensive perfume. I forgave them too.

I could go on and on. If I continue, this chapter will be a book all by itself. People always and probably always will have something to say. Just so quick to judge and tear others down. That's not how it should be. And social media has not made it any better. We live our lives out in the open for the world to see. We share our ups and downs, good days and not so good days. Many are just searching for a listening ear, looking for someone to connect with who can feel what we are sharing. The word "congratulations" is important. We should delight in the celebration of others. We never know who needs to hear it. One good word or meme could really make the world of difference to someone. Some don't share because they fear the judgement of others.

We all have demons! Now, I didn't say that we are all demons. I said we all have them. Your demon(s) may differ from those of others because no two people are the same ... not even identical twins. Two people with the same or similar issues will deal their hurt in different ways. So many cry and suffer in silence because it is so hard to talk to people. It's especially hard when you are not sure how to tell someone what's truly going on with you. Been there! When our loved ones talk, are we truly listening? Are we listening to hear or to respond? Are we focusing on the content or just listening for a point where we can jump in and tell them about us or what we think? This is not the time to think about ourselves; it's time to open our ears and hearts and close our mouths. This is the time to listen with both ears and involve your heart.

Pain is serious. Hurt is deep. Life is short. We have no idea when, where, or how we are going to leave this earth. However, one thing is certain ... we will leave. No one can or will physically live forever. Taking a few minutes to actually listen to someone can save a life. My friend had his own way of dealing with his pain. He dealt with it as best he could. But he was a praying man. Having lost his dear mother to cancer a year prior was tough for him. He fought behind closed doors. He fought when no one else was watching. But his demon had been one that plagued him for over 20 years. His substance dependency was one he could not shake. But that was his own personal fight that he only shared with a few. Who are we to judge? We each have something that we are having trouble with. It can also cause our lives to spiral out of control. Your demons have a name too! We all have things about ourselves that we are not proud of. And many are afraid to tell anyone for fear of being judged. Those we love and care about should be able to talk to us and not worry about hearing it again from someone else.

Who are we to judge? Right now you have a secret and you are afraid that if someone finds out they will tell everyone and make you look bad, but does it really matter how we look to others? No. Truthfully it only matters how we look to God. We should strive daily to please God and not man. I know it's hard to do because we have often sought the approval of our peers not considering the one who truly matters. He is the only one who can change the course of our day. Our lives are in the hands of God, but we care more about these living, breathing souls that walk around dealing with their own demons.

Have you ever said or thought about something in your mind and then heard "SO"? Well, guess what ... that happened to me. That was my inner voice. We all have an inner voice. But be careful, not every voice comes from God. If that voice is telling you to harm yourself or others, pray against it. We have work to do. *"At some point in your life you must change. God gives us each day to get better not worse."* **D. Denice Hazell** That's my mommy! I love her and all that she has taught me.

Send an encouraging word to someone you haven't heard from in a while. You never know how it will affect them.
As I sit here, pulling myself together, all I feel is gratefulness. No one could have told me a year ago that this would be my life. I truly allowed the enemy to make me believe that I had lost it all. But it was the love of God and the impartation of the Holy Spirit in my life that brought me this far. When people looked at me, they saw this smile, but behind it was so much pain and unhappiness. I was spiralling out of control. I had built up this facade of pleasantness that suggested my home life was magical ... it was, with my children. Journaling about my experiences brought me a long way. Writing down my pain forced me to look at my life from all angles. Even Though I never imagined my life like this, I chose to learn from it. I learned that my life is precious no matter what I face in it. I know that through life's ups and downs we gain wisdom and strength. It's up to me to make the best of it. Once I learned the promises of God, I knew I had a purpose. And so do you.

I pray that what I have shared with you blesses you in many ways. As painful as it was at times, I still found a reason to smile. I smile each time I think of how far God has brought me. Glory to God! I am happier now than I have been in years. No more worrying about people, places or things. No more worrying about situations out of my control. I decided to give my life to Christ. I decided to let it all go and just allow God to be God. No more trying to be the fixer, the manager, the one in control. I'm just going to give each day to my Heavenly Father and allow His miracles to work in my life. We should all find a reason to smile in any situation. No matter how painful, smile through it. Your smile may be the umbrella on some else's rainy day. Smile through the pain. I did.

The End

About the Author

Deneen J Majors was born and raised in Norfolk, Va. She graduated from NSU with a BS in Business with an emphasis in Marketing. She is also a graduate of Wards Corner Beauty Academy.

Deneen is a proud mom of 5; Antonio "Lil Smiley" Morris, Brandon Elliott, Taryn Majors, Antonio Patterson and Angel Patterson. She absolutely loves being a mom and grandma

She is the sister of Marqueta Harris aka Marqueta Plum Jenkins, Jason Hardy (d) 1976-2001, Joe Plum Jr, Antonio "Apollo da Kyng" Plum, Trena, Tonya, Meka and Junie her siblings from God whom she loves dearly and grateful that they treat her like one of them.

Deneen also has a million cousins that she loves, and this book would be a mile thick if they were all listed!

Deneen is also owner and operator at Major Creations Hair Studio. She is a Health and Wellness coach and currently owns a Total Life Changes business. Deneen also the Owner of Get Majored Apparel featuring Major Moves Wear.

She is focused and determined to make a difference for her children and grandchildren.

If this book has been a blessing you can email Deneen @ Smilingthruthepain757@gmail.com to let her know!

www.ingramcontent.com/pod-product-compliance
Lightning Source LLC
LaVergne TN
LVHW051158080426
835508LV00021B/2697